LOST AND FOUND

Mia and Murray s Beach Ball Adventure

To

Harry + Robin

hope you enjoy reading
Mia + Murrays adventure

Love Ellys xxx

Written By

Ellys Watts

Mia and Murray were two best friends who loved nothing more than spending their days at the beach. They would run around, chasing each other and playing with their favorite toy, a bright yellow tennis ball. They loved how it bounced and rolled in the sand, and how they could catch it between their teeth and tug it back and forth.

1

2

One sunny day, while they were playing on the beach, the ball bounced away from them and rolled down towards the water. Mia and Murray ran after it, but just as they were about to catch it, a big wave washed it away. They watched in horror as the ball disappeared into the sea.

4

Mia and Murray were devastated. They had never lost their favorite toy before, and they didn't know what to do. They searched the beach frantically, but the ball was nowhere to be found. They were about to give up when they saw a group of seagulls flying overhead.

"Maybe they can help us find our ball," Murray suggested.

6

Mia and Murray ran over to the seagulls and asked if they had seen their ball. The seagulls looked at them skeptically, but they agreed to help. They flew over the water, scanning the waves and calling out to each other. But after an hour of searching, they still hadn't found the ball.

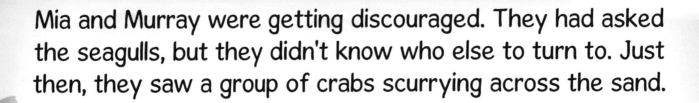

Mia and Murray were getting discouraged. They had asked the seagulls, but they didn't know who else to turn to. Just then, they saw a group of crabs scurrying across the sand.

"Maybe they can help us," Mia said hopefully.

Mia and Murray ran over to the crabs and asked if they had seen their ball. The crabs looked at them with their beady little eyes, but they agreed to help. They scurried across the beach, searching under rocks and in the tide pools. But after an hour of searching, they still hadn't found the ball.

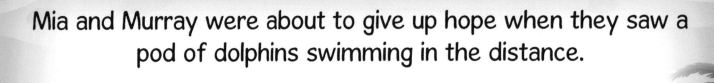

Mia and Murray were about to give up hope when they saw a pod of dolphins swimming in the distance.

"Maybe they can help us," Murray said excitedly.

Mia and Murray ran over to the water and called out to the dolphins. The dolphins looked at them curiously, but they agreed to help. They dove under the water, searching the depths for the ball. But after an hour of searching, they still hadn't found the ball.

13

14

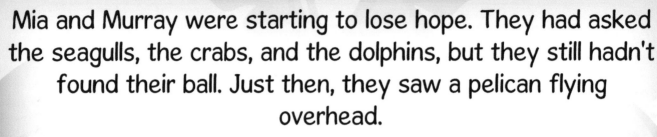

Mia and Murray were starting to lose hope. They had asked the seagulls, the crabs, and the dolphins, but they still hadn't found their ball. Just then, they saw a pelican flying overhead.

"Maybe he can help us," Mia said hopefully.

15

Mia and Murray ran over to the pelican and asked if he had seen their ball. The pelican looked at them with his big beak, but he agreed to help. He flew high into the sky, scanning the beach and the water. And finally, after what seemed like hours of searching, he spotted something yellow floating in the water.

"It's your ball!" he called out to Mia and Murray.

18

Mia and Murray were overjoyed. They ran over to where the pelican had pointed, and sure enough, there was their ball, floating in the water. They jumped in and swam towards it, and just as they were about to grab it, a big wave washed it away again

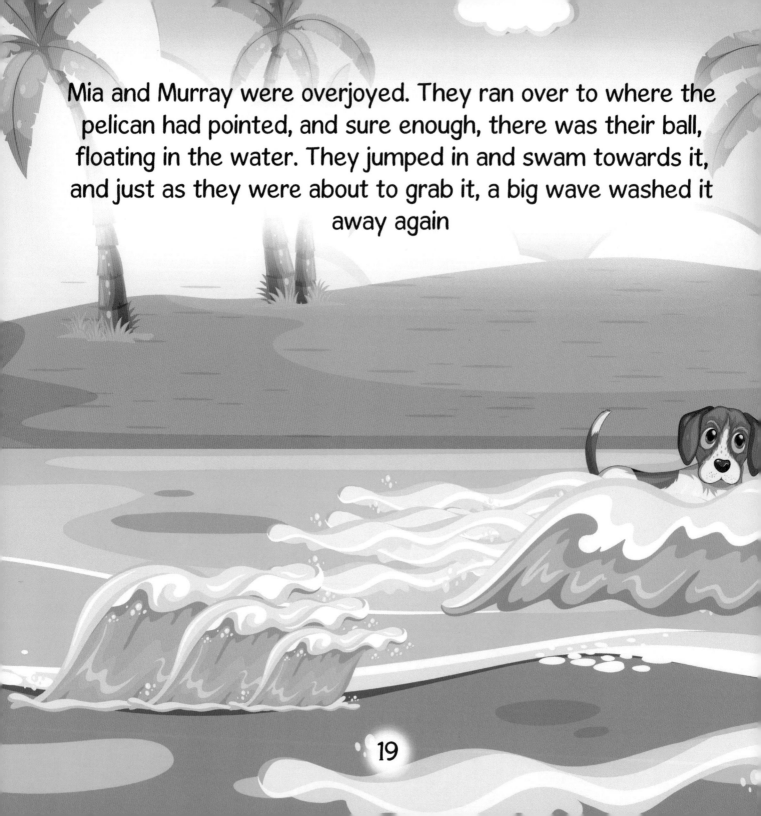

Mia and Murray chased after the ball, swimming as fast as they could. They were almost at the ball when they saw a big shadow looming beneath them.

"It's a shark!" Murray cried out.

But before they could swim away, the shadow passed them by, revealing a friendly whale. The whale had seen Mia and Murray's predicament and decided to help. The whale used its powerful tail to push the ball back towards the shore, where Mia and Murray could reach it.

Mia and Murray were ecstatic. They had their favorite toy back, thanks to the help of all the animals they had asked for assistance. They thanked the pelican, the dolphins, the crabs, and the seagulls, and of course, the friendly whale who had saved the day.

As they ran back up the beach, ball in tow, Mia and Murray realized that they had made some new friends that day. They had learned that sometimes, it's okay to ask for help, and that there are kind animals out there willing to lend a hand (or a tail) when you need it.

From that day forward, Mia and Murray continued to enjoy their days at the beach, but they were more grateful for the company of all the creatures that called it home. And whenever they saw one of their new friends, they would wag their tails and give them a friendly bark, knowing that they had all shared a special moment together.

29

THE END

Printed in Great Britain
by Amazon